MICHAEL GOW is a writer and director. His writing credits for stage, screen and radio are extensive. His writing credits include the multi-award winning play *Away*, *The Kid*, *On Top of the World*, *Europe*, *1841*, *Furious*, *Sweet Phoebe*, *Live Acts on Stage*, *The Fortunes of Richard Mahony* and *Toy Symphony*. He currently holds the role of Artistic Director of Queensland Theatre Company, where his credits include *Who's Afraid of Virginia Woolf?*, *John Gabriel Borkman*, *Private Fears in Public Places*, *Private Lives* (co-production with State Theatre of South Australia), *Away* (co-production with Griffin Theatre), *Oedipus the King*, *The Venetian Twins*, *The Cherry Orchard*, *The Real Inspector Hound*, *Black Comedy*, *Phedra*, *We Were Dancing*, *The Fortunes of Richard Mahony* (co-production with Playbox), *Cooking with Elvis*, *Bag O' Marbles*, *The Tragedy of King Richard III* (collaboration with The Bell Shakespeare Company), *The Tragedy of King Richard the Second*, *Buried Child*, *Dirt*, *Fred*, *Shopping & F$$$ing*, *Mrs Warren's Profession*, *The Skin of Our Teeth* and *XPO—The Human Factor*. He has also worked as a director for Sydney Theatre Company, where he was Associate Director from 1991 to 1993, Company B, Black Swan Theatre Company, Griffin Theatre Company, State Theatre Company of South Australia, Australian Theatre for Young People, Playbox, Opera Australia, Sydney Festival and Adelaide Festival.

Richard Roxburgh as Roland and Monica Maughan as Mrs Walkham in the 2007 Company B production in Sydney. *(Photo: Heidrun Löhr)*

Toy Symphony

Michael Gow

Currency Press, Sydney

CURRENCY PLAYS

First published in 2008
by Currency Press Pty Ltd,
PO Box 2287, Strawberry Hills, NSW, 2012, Australia
enquiries@currency.com.au
www.currency.com.au

Reprinted 2015

Cataloguing-in-publication data for this title is available from the National Library of Australia website: www.nla.gov.au

Typeset by Dean Nottle for Currency Press.
Printed by Fineline Print & Copy Service, St Peters, NSW.
Cover design by Laura McLean, Currency Press.Cover shows Richard Roxburgh as Roland in the 2007 Company B production. Photo: (Photo: Heidrun Löhr)

Contents

I'm having amnesia and déjà vu at the same time.

Steven Wright

Mind the Gap

Neil Armfield

Michael Gow and I grew up on either side of the same town. He in Como, me in Concord. We both started infants school in 1960 and did the HSC in '72 at Jannali and Homebush Boys' High Schools respectively. At school we were both called the same names that are given to the gentler boys by the footy heroes in the playground, we both experienced the premature death to leukaemia of someone close to us—for Michael his best friend David, for me my brother Ian. At Sydney Uni we fell into the fabulous refuge of SUDS (Sydney University Drama Society) and, having serious fun doing plays, our professional development began. We acted together occasionally (he was much better) and I directed Michael in our last SUDS show in 1979, the same year that we began parallel professional careers. In 1986 I directed Michael's great play *Away* at Melbourne's Playbox, in 1988 he wrote the screenplay for *Edens Lost* that I directed, and we worked together on a mini-series from Patrick White's *The Tree of Man* that has never been produced. In 1991 a mutual friend was living in my house in Leichhardt when her boyfriend's mate's dog Phoebe, that they had been minding while the mate was overseas, went missing. Thus began a chain of events that informed Michael's play *Sweet Phoebe* and most recently, *Toy Symphony*.

I suppose I list all of the above information as a way of saying that I feel very (at times uncomfortably) close to the world of this play, and, I guess, singularly qualified to direct it! Ultimately, of course, this is all privileged information and the test of the play will be how it stands on its own terms.

In a *Sunday Arts* interview with Virginia Trioli last week, the great comic Magda Szubanski offered the comment that we in Australia fight our suburban past but are also defined by it and that any artist at some point has to work from it because it has made us who we are. And I realised that Michael has written a profoundly personal and honest work about the collapse of the suburban dream. A work about both the power and the bastardry of the artist. What's fascinating is the way the play apparently changes shape, morphing two or three times along the way into what can seem to be another kind of play altogether.

I love that. And that the whole play works through action which is analogous to the central experience of the blockage and flow of creativity.

It's two weeks before our first audience we're still finding the direction, the humour, the pain of the work. It's exciting and difficult fun. It comes straight from the heart.

The above is a note I wrote for the program of the Company B premiere of *Toy Symphony* at Belvoir St Theatre in 2007. It's written at the most vulnerable time in rehearsal before you really know what you've got on your hands and everything is informed by a kind of wilful optimism that it will all turn out ok! Like many directors about to open a new play, I'm using the note as a way of anticipating criticism and shoring up our exposed flanks.

Nothing had prepared us for the pleasure that *Toy Symphony* would give people in the theatre. As always, it's during the previews that patterns emerge and you carefully begin to form your expectations for the First Night.

Early on in rehearsal Roland's great opening monologue had ceased to be funny. After initial blocking where the emotional and physical shape was explored, and the movement of thought mapped, I said to Richard 'It's now kind of undirectable: you will know how to perform this only when there's a house in—we will go through weeks of this seeming like torture as you chase evaporating rehearsal room laughs—it will all change totally with an audience'. For once, I was exactly right. Richard Roxburgh is an actor who can smell an audience's hope. Michael knows that instinct in a great actor because he's been one. That's why he writes so well for them to let rip in performance—which is just what happened at Belvoir St. Immediately.

Peter Kingston, who directed the historic premiere of *Away* for Griffin in 1986, sat in the front row of our second preview: he stretched back and just received the play. He said 'It was like this with *Away*—we thought we were doing a story about a boy dying. Then audiences came and told us what this play was'.

The gap between the rehearsal experience and the performed show can sometimes appear very large indeed. For instance, there had been scenes that seemed quite fragile, that had changed almost daily in rehearsal. Michael had been unsure of the tone of nearly all the school and childhood scenes of Roland's past (except for the two great classroom scenes—they never changed): just how far the cartoon of memory could stretch; how to achieve the balance, especially for Nick Eglitis (as he became) and Steve Gooding; how to weave them through the developing Act 1 spine—the series of sessions with his therapist, Nina. Unlike other parts of the play, the text for these scenes remained mutable, with great input from the rehearsal room floor, right up to Opening. But once we hit the audience, they seemed so solid! The alchemy of performance rendered those scenes as if they'd always been thus … they were suddenly classical.

Over the course of that first season the breadth and the hidden architecture of the play could be more and more felt. I loved the freshness, the sense of delight in which audiences would be bounced from one surprise to the next. Tom Stoppard turned up at one show and quietly admired 'One senses this playwright has a few tricks up his sleeve'.

Particularly special were the schools' performances. I felt proud of the respect the play harbours for teachers—well, those very special ones who reach through and change your life—and the sense that who you are is somehow formed in the classroom and playground at school. An amazing thing for kids to apprehend! It was talking to the kids after one show that I realised that *Toy Symphony* is really a kind of classic quest: our Odysseus lost, despairing, abandoning the world, is finally led back to it by a simple action of grace and the redemptive power of art.

I marvel at the apparent miracle that this play, drawn I know so much from the chaos of a life lived, is ultimately a work of such original, delicate, yet secure structure and deep poetic resonance.

But that, precisely, is Michael's gift.

Sydney
April 2008

Neil Armfield AO is Artistic Director of Company B Belvoir where he directed the premiere season of *Toy Symphony*.

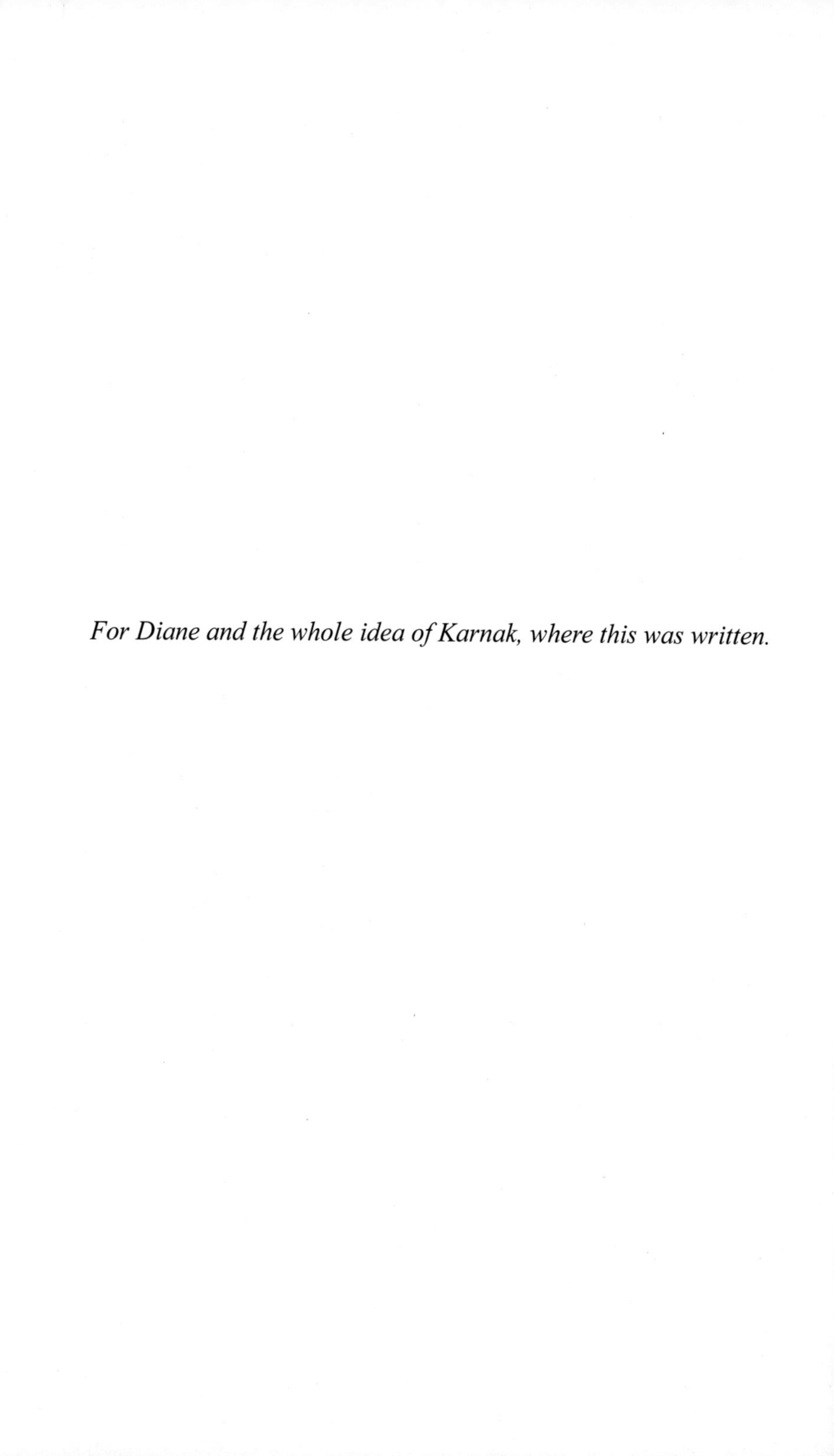

For Diane and the whole idea of Karnak, where this was written.

Toy Symphony was first produced by Company B at the Belvoir St Theatre, Sydney, on 14 November 2006 with the following cast:

NINA / JULIE PEARSON / MISS BEVERLY / LYNETTE MCKENZIE	Justine Clarke
LAWYER / HEADMASTER / DR MAYBLOOM / STEVE GOODING / MR DEVLIN / TOM / TITUS OATES / CHEKHOV	Russell Dykstra
NICK / DANIEL / ALEXANDER THE GREAT	Guy Edmonds
MRS WALKHAM / NURSE	Monica Maughan
ROLAND HENNING	Richard Roxburgh

Director, Neil Armfield
Set Design, Ralph Myers
Costume Design, Tess Schofield
Lighting Design, Damien Cooper
Composer and Sound Design, Paul Charlier
Assistant Sound Design, Michael Toisuta
Assistant Director, Michael Lutton

CHARACTERS

ROLAND
NINA, a therapist
LAWYER
MRS WALKHAM, a school teacher
HEADMASTER
JULIE, a schoolgirl
DR MAYBLOOM, a specialist
EXECUTIONER
NICOLAJS, a schoolboy
TITUS OATES
MISS BEVERLY, a school teacher
NURSE
STEVEN, a school bully
LYNETTE, a schoolgirl
MR DEVLIN, a headmaster
DANIEL, a drama student
TOM, a drug dealer
ALEXANDER THE GREAT
ANTON CHEKHOV

ACT ONE

The writer ROLAND HENNING *finds himself in the consulting room of a therapist,* NINA.

NINA: What I'm interested in is clarity, in a better understanding of whatever we're afraid of—

ROLAND: Yes, uh-huh—

NINA: —what it is that's stopping us doing what it is we want to do—

ROLAND: Uh-huh, yes.

NINA: —identifying thinking or behaviour that is clearly negative, destructive—

ROLAND: Uh-huh, right, clarity, yes.

NINA: —So that we know it better, the fear, the pressure—

ROLAND: Okay look, I can't write. Save a lot of time, straight to it, can't write. That's pretty clear, don't you think?

NINA: Roland, we know you can write. There's a body of work, you have a reputation. But, well, this is interesting, this is what I'm talking about. For some reason, you currently believe, for whatever reason, you *believe* you can't write.

ROLAND: Uh-huh.

NINA: And it's that kind of thinking that might be a good place to start. Anyone dealing with a creative block can start to look at—

ROLAND: No. No. This isn't writer's... thing, no.

NINA: Writer's...?

ROLAND: You know.

NINA: Writer's...?

ROLAND: I don't have... it's not that. Let's just get that—

NINA: You mean writer's block?

ROLAND: There you are, you see.

NINA: I didn't actually use that term.

ROLAND: Maybe not, not out loud, but it's still there, underneath. See Dr...?

NINA: Nina.

ROLAND: Nina, if this is going to work, if, and I really don't, I'm not sure, really, if there's any point and this isn't you, no, I have the greatest, I'm sure you're terrific, you're the one who's read *The Interpretation of Dreams* or you saw your grandfather naked when you were six and you have devoted your life to understanding the effect that had, I see that, but let me be perfectly clear I do not have writer's…

NINA: Writer's…

ROLAND: I told you.

NINA: Writer's…?

ROLAND: Okay, uh-huh. This is a technique, getting me to admit I have a problem, and then if I admit it then I have it. But I told you. I don't have writer's… block, there I said it.

NINA: Roland, I didn't say—

ROLAND: And I mean writer's… thing, I mean it's such a meaningless term anyway, a Hollywood fiction, a monumental cliché and if that's how you're going to, if you think that's how you're going to whatever it is you intend doing or attempting, by removing this… block, as if, as if there's this there's this river, that comes bubbling up from the deep, way down in the Permian layers, thrusting up through the ancient strata, forced up by the internal forces, pressures, and it spills out, it bursts out into the dazzling light on the slopes of some painfully clear, bright mountainside and runs down this upper slope, this high country all clean and clear and sparkling like a Norsca ad, pure inspiration running over stones, through rapids, until it reaches the tree line. Then, there, it starts to wander through dank forests, spilling over mossy rocks and forming still, deep pools full of incredibly clear-sighted fish and visionary yabbies, carving out ravines all verdurous and gloomy with the slowly forming thoughts, just inklings of works of art. And then our river reaches the edge of the mountain ridge and now it plunges out of this high country, roaring over cliffs, cataracts, thundering over the edge of the falls, down into conscious valleys, deep chasms of impulse and first ideas, flowing on through steep gorges and wild, white water, churning up basic structures. It's violent and dangerous but finally it begins to slow down because it's reached the plains where there's habitation, creative cities full of neo-classical libraries and museums with all the previous works and commentaries and interpretations on show so they can be admired, where you can find inspiration and study whatever you need to build your own work. And after the city, it flows even more slowly so the happy peasants can draw the water from the river in their intricate, ancient watering devices to nourish the fields where the new works have been sown and where they start to grow. And then, at last, the river reaches the delta and splits into a dozen different tributaries and the mud is incredibly fertile and masterpieces spring up almost without anyone having to do any work and then our weary river winds safely out into the vast ocean, stately, grand, with loud Beethoven playing, out to where Leviathan lives, brooding at the bottom, sending up the simplest, grandest thoughts to keep the ocean busy. And then the sun draws up the water and fat clouds form, thundering with thought so basic it's before thought, chthonic thunderheads. And the clouds drift towards the mountains and get snagged and it rains and the water tumbles down through fissures deep into the earth and it all starts over again and again and again and suddenly. Across our river— bang. Warragamba Dam. And the flow is stopped. It's blocked. By a block, the river is blocked by whatever; impotence, fear of failure, fear of success, fear of death, whatever. And I struggle helplessly with that, until you come along, with the psycho-cavalry and you help me work it through until one day, through persistence and 'I will not be defeated' and 'I am a valuable person' and I don't know, the workings of grace, you fly in like dambusters and drop your bouncing therapeutic bomb and it explodes and the wall collapses and water pours out and floods the towns downstream, and everything gets washed away and cleared away and swept away and new levels of fertile mud are deposited and the river is flowing again. And. I'm saved. Now. If that's how you, if that's what I'm paying a hundred and forty dollars an hour for well… you know. I don't think…

He breaks down.

NINA: Roland, do you need—?

She hands him a box of tissues, he snaps out of it.

ROLAND: I'm fine, I faked that, it's easy to do, been around actors long enough, so breaking down, the sobbing confession or the really sad moment in my past that's caused this isn't going to happen either, so there's no point… I won't be… okay? And don't expect me to imagine myself as a ten-year-old either, I'm not doing that, don't buy that for a minute, talk to my ten-year-old self, or relive teenage traumas so they lose their power, uh-uh, uh-uh. Is that all… all of that, you know, clear? It's not me, that's all. Not me.

Pause.

NINA: So why are you here?

ROLAND: A friend thought I should come and see you. This friend is worried, he's really worried, he's always worried about me, he's great, his name's Jake, he's my best, and he worries and he's thinking of moving to New York so he worries even more, so he said he thought it would be a good idea to see someone like you.

NINA: But you made the decision to see me.

ROLAND: Well yes, but Jake you see, well he's feeling guilty you see, he feels a little responsible for some of what's been happening. He introduced me to this woman who was babysitting a dog that belonged to friends of hers.

NINA: A dog?

ROLAND: [*he looks at her for a moment, then goes on*] She's a friend, was a friend of Jake's. The dog went missing, ran away, got stolen and she went crazy trying to find it again. She told me about what happened and then I wrote a play about it, which is where you might say this started this, lack of… me not…

NINA: But, Roland, you made the appointment, so no matter how guilty your friend was feeling, no matter how worried, you made the call—

ROLAND: Uh-huh—

NINA: —there was a desire, a need on your part, to come here. You've decided you can't write, then you tell me what you don't want, what you're not going to do, make fun of what I'm trying to get started. Then you tell me you're only here to make someone else feel better. I don't know why you're here. You may as well pay yourself a hundred and forty dollars an hour and stay home as far as I can see.

ROLAND: That's probably very true, I thought it would be a mistake, but Jake kept at me—

NINA: So what, you have no control over your friend's concerns? He worries, you react? That might be an interesting place to start any kind of work—

ROLAND: He's my friend, it matters, what he thinks matters, maybe you don't have anyone to worry about you, you've sorted everyone out in your life.

NINA: Oh, I have someone to worry about me. And I can also be honest about the things that concern me. Sorry, but I'm not going to sit here and get boxed into some personal view you have about me and my kind. Before we even start. How can I proceed if that's where we start from? You must want to be here, you must want to address something, but so far, I have no idea. You have an advantage over a lot of the people I see. Most of them can't put even a few words together that gives even the vaguest sense of what they think, feel. I'd say you have language in your grip and that's wonderful. But you also use your command of language to hide, to avoid. You're here for some reason, even if you don't want to admit what it is. You want something badly. So badly you're prepared to do anything, even something you think is as ridiculous as coming here. Yes?

ROLAND: Well…

NINA: You're in trouble, Roland. You're clearly in denial about something, if that's not sounding too much like a cliché shrink talking. Denial. About your work, your life, something. You're in trouble. I know you're in trouble because… I'll just say it, come out and say it. What's your drug of choice, Roland? There's a slight glassiness, there's irritability, as well as the words, this torrent, this wall of words. You're hiding from something, that's what any substance abuse is about—No wonder Jake's worried about you.

ROLAND: Okay okay—

NINA: But if we're going to start any kind of work, we have to start with where you are right now. Before we start to even think about writing. So, what? I assume some amphetamine, or coke is it? Worse?

Silence.

At this point, at any point, you can leave. You can get up and leave, angry at my presumption, every right. Or. We could start. Talking.

Silence.

ROLAND: Okay.

NINA: Yes?

Pause.

ROLAND: So have you read *The Interpretation of Dreams*?
NINA: As a matter of fact, Roland, I have.
ROLAND: Okay. Good. That's something. [*Pause.*] That's a start.

♦♦♦♦♦

ROLAND *is in the office of an eminent copyright* LAWYER.

LAWYER: What I'd like you to do is think of the telephone book. This I think will make your position, our position, quite clear. As a model it is open to dispute, there are challenges, but I believe it still holds good. Think of the telephone book.
ROLAND: The telephone book, yes, I'm thinking of the telephone book.
LAWYER: The phone book. You've got the *white* pages. The white *pages*; a list of all telephone subscribers arranged alphabetically. And the *yellow* pages. All the material arranged under subject headings, yes? Now. There's no copyright on the white pages, the white pages are not subject to copyright because, the alphabet, as a way of, it's a method in use since whichever smart Phoenician invented the alphabet. So. *White* pages. That's your raw material, that's the life, the event, the experience. Yes?
ROLAND: Yes.
LAWYER: Now. *Yellow* pages. In compiling the *yellow* pages, someone, someone or *other* some*where* came up with the subject headings under which all businesses are listed. Someone *decided*, say, they made the choice, that doctors would be listed under Medical Practitioners and not Doctors. Evening wear hire, it says 'see Bridal and Evening Wear Hire'. And within these listings there is art work, graphics, layout. The whole of the yellow pages phone book is the result of choice, decisions have been made, a shape has been imposed on raw material, yes? There's your work of art, your play, novel, film, whathaveyou. And on that material there is, of course, copyright. The yellow pages. Is subject. To copyright. Now our litigious friend's original experience, the missing dog and the search and eventual discovery of the dog, even though a small part of it was written down on paper, the notes that she made, that is white pages stuff, mere listing of events, especially, *especially* as everyone as you say, many, *many* people, had heard it as well in the same way, the same form. Public domain, that's what that is. Out. There. Whereas

your version, your *play* is yellow pages country. You've done what you, you've waved your magic wand over the raw material, you've brought something uniquely yours, your own product, into being. Completely clear, beyond, no doubt.

ROLAND: None?

LAWYER: No.

ROLAND: So this injunction she's taken out, to stop the play—?

LAWYER: Will be lifted.

ROLAND: And if it isn't?

LAWYER: But it will be.

ROLAND: But if it isn't? And they go on rehearsing and opening night comes and there's still this injunction.

LAWYER: Then a sheriff will come to the theatre and use the power of the court to prevent the performance taking place.

ROLAND: A sheriff?

LAWYER: Or he will halt the play if the performance has begun. But that will not happen. I am assured that you have done only what any writer does, takes material that has common currency and turned it into a literary work. I have no doubt at all that this injunction will be lifted.

Pause.

ROLAND: Okay. [*Pause.*] Okay. [*Pause.*] My problem is, this play, the play I wrote, she claims I stole it from her. Yes?

LAWYER: That's correct.

ROLAND: And you feel we can prove that's not the case.

LAWYER: We have proven that, *you* have proven that. All the work you've, the comparative analysis of your play and her story, proves that.

ROLAND: That's what we've proven, yes. But is it true?

LAWYER: Yes it is, Mr Henning.

ROLAND: Oh, I know we've proven, *legally*, that I didn't steal it. And you're convinced I didn't.

LAWYER: I am.

ROLAND: But I did.

LAWYER: We know now you did not. Like any artist you used material that was freely available—

ROLAND: What if, even though she told a lot of people, she told *me*, deliberately, so that I would write about it.

LAWYER: I'm not sure…

ROLAND: She maybe, maybe she entrusted it to me in a particular way, *knowing* I would write about it. Yes?

Pause.

LAWYER: Possibly.

ROLAND: And I did, that's exactly what I did. Well no not exactly, that's the problem, I changed things, ran with it. And she didn't like the way it turned out. You see, she doesn't want money, does she?

LAWYER: Not in the first instance.

ROLAND: She doesn't want a credit.

LAWYER: No, she wants the play stopped.

ROLAND: Because?

LAWYER: Her claim is you stole the idea—

ROLAND: That's what she's saying now. And I'm admitting I did, okay, I'm confessing to you that I did that.

LAWYER: I don't really need to hear—

ROLAND: But. But. Why is she really doing this? Why has she mounted this case? Technically, as we keep saying, the case she's mounting doesn't hold up, you can't steal a story that everyone's heard, we know that thanks to our friend the telephone book. As a person, as an individual, she's perfectly nice, a nice woman, I quite like her. But. She doesn't have much of a grip on her life you see, she's got no real sense of purpose, okay? Like a lot of us. But. She was hoping, this is what I think, she was hoping my play would somehow redeem, or or transfigure the experience she had. But my play didn't exactly follow her story, give her story meaning, put her, put the basically ridiculous story of what she went through in a heroic, or, well, meaningful light on stage, but instead it became a different, difficult, not flattering, that's the point, not flattering play that I wrote. No redemption. And that is very difficult for her, she feels betrayed. She must. Betrayed, hurt, angry. And her feelings, those feelings… I think she wants to punish. Me. She's already been to the papers, to embarrass me. Now she's taken out an injunction that we know she can't win. So what will she do next? I have this sense. There's more.

Pause.

LAWYER: She could argue some kind of breach of trust in some moral sense.

ROLAND: Would she have, would that stand up?

LAWYER: Again, the case would be weak.

ROLAND: It doesn't matter how weak. If she fails on the injunction, I suspect, the next step is some kind of, as you say, moral…

LAWYER: High dudgeon, that's what it would it be, yes. As you say, she's already been to the papers, there's a deal of sympathy for her out there, some support for her taking out this injunction. You're successful in your field. There's always someone pleased to see someone in your position take a fall. Moral outrage, victimhood, would keep the story alive.

ROLAND: There you are. There. You are.

LAWYER: This puts a, a—

ROLAND: New twist, doesn't it?

Silence.

LAWYER: I see.

ROLAND: How do we stop it now? How do we nail a lid on it? On her?

LAWYER: Is that what you want to do?

ROLAND: I don't want to answer the charge she's made against me. She tried to shut me up. So what I want is to shut her up. Instead.

Pause.

LAWYER: Our defamation laws are quite strict.

ROLAND: Yes?

LAWYER: Yes. We could inform her that unless the injunction is lifted and this matter is dropped immediately, she will have defamed you, your honour, integrity, by making these claims.

ROLAND: We could do that?

LAWYER: It would certainly be a decisive step.

ROLAND: You see, that's what I want. I want to take a decisive step.

LAWYER: It is, as it were, *o*ffensive, rather than *de*fensive.

ROLAND: Attack.

LAWYER: You could put it like that.

ROLAND: You don't like it, you think this is too…

LAWYER: It doesn't answer the question to hand. Nothing is refuted, nothing is defended. She will withdraw the injunction, but not because she sees her case is flawed, but because she feels…

ROLAND: Threatened?

LAWYER: The response would contain some degree of intimidation.

ROLAND: I want her silenced. I will not be silenced, no. It's she who must be silenced. It disappoints you I know.

LAWYER: It's not about what I want, Mr Henning. It's about what you want. If that is what you instruct me to do, then I will do it.

ROLAND: Do it. I want her to feel panic. I want her to be shaken. And silenced.

♦♦♦♦♦

In the therapist's room.

NINA: And the play went ahead?

ROLAND: It did.

NINA: No more from the woman?

ROLAND: Nothing. Shut her up.

NINA: You got what you wanted?

ROLAND: Yes.

NINA: And you felt… satisfaction?

ROLAND: For a minute.

NINA: Can I ask? You proved you hadn't stolen her story, you started out proving that. How did you do that?

ROLAND: I went through every line of dialogue in the play, compared it with, with what she wrote down, her *version*, line by line, methodically worked through it all, every draft. There wasn't a phrase that suggested, in the smallest way, that behind my play there was anything she herself wrote.

NINA: You went through your work that closely?

ROLAND: Line by line, phrase by phrase, the entire script, all the drafts. Looking for what was it? 'Any distinctive linguistic patterns' that she could argue I took.

NINA: How did that feel, doing that?

ROLAND: It felt… I don't know. I just did it.

NINA: Had you done it before, looked at your work that way before?

ROLAND: No.

NINA: So it was new experience. How did that feel?

Pause.

ROLAND: I don't remember.

NINA: Remember now, try and remember now.

ROLAND: I can't.

NINA: Just think about it.

ROLAND: I mean I don't think I felt anything, I was so determined to get her off my back.

NINA: Try. Think back. You're examining your work, looking for something that will, well maybe, incriminate you. Tell me what you're feeling.

ROLAND: Ahh…

NINA: It's difficult.

ROLAND: Yes.

NINA: What are you thinking, what are you seeing, feeling?

Pause.

ROLAND: It's like, I'm wandering through my own brain with a smoking torch, scorching everything I'm looking at.

NINA: Yes. Good, thank you, good. You can relax. You're feeling…

ROLAND: Dandy, just, you know… extreme panic, but apart from that.

NINA: Yes. Looking at your work in that way…

ROLAND: Not even seeing how…

NINA: What?

ROLAND: The damage.

NINA: You think it did you damage?

ROLAND: I don't write, I spent a lot of money on speed and coke, so yes.

NINA: How, do you think? Was the damage done?

ROLAND: I became… self-conscious. Of my own voice, style, instincts, impulses. Yes. So self-aware that now I can't do anything without questioning it. And when you question your basic instincts that closely, they seize up. Paralysis.

NINA: Good analysis.

ROLAND: I think it's pretty accurate.

NINA: Some people have described the creative act as if being in a trance, someone said it's like sleepwalking, which I think is a good, an interesting analogy. Because if someone is sleepwalking you don't wake them. There's a possibility of shock, a shock to the… being suddenly brought out of that state to total awareness. The artist needs to be left in a state that's not fully awake in the day to day reality. And what you did for that lawyer brought you out of that state to… well, like you were forever wide awake, looking over your own shoulder while you were working.

Pause.

Richard Roxburgh as Roland and Justine Clarke as Nina in the 2007 Company B production in Sydney. (Photo: Heidrun Löhr)

ROLAND: Goethe.
NINA: I'm sorry?
ROLAND: It was Goethe who said the creative act is like sleepwalking.
NINA: Thank you.
ROLAND: So she's shut me up after all. Maybe for good.
NINA: I don't believe that.
ROLAND: You haven't asked me if I feel guilty.
NINA: For what?
ROLAND: The way I shut her up.
NINA: Do you?
ROLAND: No.
NINA: Uh-huh.
ROLAND: I was just checking.
NINA: That I wasn't grabbing the most obvious—
ROLAND: Exactly—
NINA: —typical shrink response, guilt is paralysing you, it's guilt—
ROLAND: Exactly, 'I feel guilt therefore I can't write'.
NINA: May as well say you've got writer's block.
ROLAND: Exactly.
NINA: Okay. Good. Thank you. I'd like to think about, I know this will be hard, you've indicated your aversion to this kind of thing, but next week I'd like you to talk about a time when you were maybe, a time when you were free of this self-consciousness.
ROLAND: My childhood?
NINA: If that's the period of your life you first think of.
ROLAND: It is, damn it.

NINA *laughs.*

What?
NINA: Nothing. If you can, if you want to go there, that is the time we should, maybe, address.

♦♦♦♦♦

MRS WALKHAM, *a middle-aged primary school teacher, comes on. She brings some kind of projector, slide, or overhead. She looks around for a power point, pulls the lamp cord out, sudden darkness.*

MRS WALKHAM: Oh.

She manages to get the lamp cord back on, light again. She brings the projector cord to the power point, takes the lamp cord out, feels her way to putting the projector cord in, feels her way along the cord to the projector and turns it on. She begins a talk illustrated with maps, diagrams, charts and slides.

Now 5A, eyes to the front, quiet as mice. We're going to hear about the place where we live. Como. Our suburb is situated twenty miles south of the Sydney General Post Office in the Sutherland Shire. The Shire itself covers one hundred and forty-three square miles. It stretches from Botany Bay and the Georges River in the north to the Port Hacking River and the Royal National Park in the south.

The Sutherland Shire is known as the birthplace of Australia. Captain Cook had been sent to the Pacific by the Royal Geographic Society to help scientists watch the planet Venus cross the sun. This was called the transit of Venus. On this voyage he also explored the east coast of Australia. He entered Botany Bay in April 1770, and at Kurnell, the first Englishman came ashore onto this great land. Here you can see Captain Cook greeting the Aborigines in a re-enactment of his landing for the country's sesquicentenary. That means one hundred and fiftieth anniversary.

The Sutherland Shire has many associations with the past but it's very important to our future as well. At Kurnell, right on Botany Bay, right where Captain Cook landed, there's the Australian Oil Refinery, and to the west, at Lucas Heights, is the Atomic Energy Commission's nuclear reactor, researching exciting new ways to produce energy.

As well as these man-made wonders we have so much natural wonder as well. There's the Royal National Park, which is the second oldest national park in the world, after Yellowstone, in America. As well as bush there are beaches, at Cronulla and Wanda. But as well as all this, there are houses, hundreds of thousands of houses, suburbs full of houses, street after street. These suburbs grew very quickly after the Second World War. They were built by soldiers returning from the war for their new families.

And on the edge of all this suburban life there's Como. It was named by a man called James Murphy. He was looking for coal in the area. He named it after Lake Como in Italy. It was here at Como, that the railway line south from Sydney crossed the Georges River. The railway was originally built to bring coal from Bulli and Kiama. James Murphy didn't find any coal here, but once the railway line was built, people saw how pretty it was and started coming here to escape the city. They built pleasure grounds and paddle steamer cruises began on the river in the early 1900s. Here you can see one ready to depart. Look at those elegant ladies.

Many of the men who built the railway came from Italy. Many of the streets of Como still have an Italian flavour: Genoa Street, Cremona Avenue, Novara Crescent, Verona Street. And many other streets bear names from the language of the people who first lived here. Yamba, Woronora, Warraba.

As I said, after World War Two, people really began to move to the area, build their homes and start their families. In January 1950, Miss Clarice Drury opened the doors of Como West Infants School, to enrol its first seventy children. There were only two rooms in one building, but the school grew and grew as more people moved here to enjoy life in this leafy, quiet suburb.

But life hasn't always been sedate, far from it. Everyone will know what I'm talking about when I say Red Tuesday or Black Sunday, Black Friday, Ash Wednesday; terrible names for terrible days. Terrible because of bushfire. And we've had terrible fires in our own shire, nearly every year. Homes are lost, sometimes lives. Terrible days. But let's not forget, that after fire, the bush does grow back. People rebuild.

♦♦♦♦♦

Back to NINA *and* ROLAND.

NINA: Okay, good, thank you. This teacher… Mrs?
ROLAND: Walkham.
NINA: She is a strong memory for you?
ROLAND: Yes.
NINA: Her personality, her energy?
ROLAND: Her voice.
NINA: Her voice?
ROLAND: She had a beautiful voice, warm, comforting.
NINA: And that made you feel…?

ROLAND: Safe, it made me feel I was somewhere safe, that was full of interesting things.

NINA: And you were free to feel and think and express your responses to these things?

ROLAND: Yes it was all lovely and honey sandwiches and baa lambs, but look. This is where it's going to get rough, okay, this is where you'll start prescribing lithium or shock treatment. This talking cure you've been running has been really, well, it's been a great way to spend an hour a week and a better way to spend money than snorting coke. But look, here's the thing, the turning point, the snag, the stumbling block. I tell you about say, this teacher, Mrs Walkham, or the copyright lawyer I saw. Once, when I was young, I'd have been able to show you.

NINA: Show me?

ROLAND: You'd have been there. No, they'd have been here.

NINA: You can describe things very—

ROLAND: No no, it's got nothing to do with 'in your mind's eye', no. They'd have been here. Actually been here.

Pause.

NINA: I'm not sure…

ROLAND: They'd have been here, in the room. You would have seen them, heard them. In the flesh.

NINA: Okay. That's very interesting.

Pause.

ROLAND: So you've just pressed a hidden button and there's an ambulance on the way right now?

NINA: No.

ROLAND: And you'll just keep me here, distract me until they come pounding up the stairs with the tranquiliser dart?

NINA: Can I just, I need to ask… you haven't been taking anything?

ROLAND: No. Thought about it. Wanted to. But…

NINA: Good, that's good. And then, sometimes, when there's been a degree of dependence, the effect—

ROLAND: And this isn't withdrawal, I'm not having an episode, what, 'am I psychotic?' No, it's not that.

NINA: No, no, I believe you—

ROLAND: Really?
NINA: Yes Roland. I do. The time is nearly up.
ROLAND: How convenient.
NINA: Next week, I want to talk about this... what do you call it? Ability? Gift?
ROLAND: That will do.
NINA: We'll talk about it, tell me about your experience, what it was like, what it felt like, when it started.
ROLAND: And then you'll call the ambulance, right?
NINA: No.
ROLAND: Uh-huh.
NINA: No.

♦♦♦♦♦

The HEADMASTER *and some of Roland's classmates appear.*

MRS WALKHAM: 5A, quiet as mice. We're now going to recite the poem we've been learning for the Headmaster. You begin, Julie Pearson.
JULIE PEARSON: Oh to be in—
MRS WALKHAM: Uh!
JULIE PEARSON: 'Home Thoughts from Abroad' by Robert Browning.
Oh to be in England now that April's there,
And who ever wakes in England
sees some morning, unaware—
HEADMASTER: *Oh*! To be in *England*! The cry of a soul in exile! *Oh* to be in *England*. Again Julie Pearson.
JULIE PEARSON: *Oh* to be in *England*! Now that *April's* there.
HEADMASTER: For whoever wakes *where*? In?
JULIE PEARSON: *England*!
HEADMASTER: Good, sees some morning, una*ware*, go on. Who's next?

Silence.

MRS WALKHAM: Roland?

Silence.

HEADMASTER: Roland Henning. What is the next line?
ROLAND: I...
HEADMASTER: The next line.
ROLAND: Round?

HEADMASTER: Yes?

ROLAND: Elm…

HEADMASTER: Where's your mind? Were you asleep, sitting there with your eyes closed?

ROLAND: No sir, I was thinking.

HEADMASTER: What about?

ROLAND: Alexander the Great.

HEADMASTER: We're not doing history, we're doing poetry.

ROLAND: I was thinking how his men followed him wherever he went, across mountains and deserts and oceans. He got as far as India.

HEADMASTER: I don't care if he got to Hornsby. Get out here now.

ROLAND: And he was only twenty-three when he defeated the Persians.

HEADMASTER: And you won't live to see twelve. Here. Now.

ROLAND: And when Julius Caesar was thirty-three he saw a statue of Alexander and said, 'When I was his age he'd conquered the world and I still haven't done anything'.

HEADMASTER: Get up on your feet, you little mongrel. I'll give you Alexander the Great.

He's grabbed a cane but ALEXANDER THE GREAT *comes into the classroom and goes straight to the* HEADMASTER.

Who the hell are you?

ALEXANDER: Alexander of Macedon. I defeated the Persians. I burned Persepolis. I conquered the world.

HEADMASTER: Where did you come from?

ALEXANDER: Tell him.

ROLAND: The banks of the Euphrates.

ALEXANDER: Kneel.

HEADMASTER: I…

ROLAND: You better do what he says.

And the HEADMASTER *kneels before the conqueror of the world, who leaves, satisfied.*

MRS WALKHAM: Now, 5A, wasn't that a very big surprise, Alexander the Great visiting our classroom like that.

The HEADMASTER *gets up unsteadily and leaves the room.*

Now, while I check on the Headmaster, I want you to open your Social Studies books, page forty-three, The Boer War. Quickly now, nice and quiet. Yes I know it was exciting, but back to work. Read about the relief of Mafeking.

♦♦♦♦♦

ROLAND *finds himself with* DR MAYBLOOM, *a specialist in child psychology.*

ROLAND: And that's how it started. He just appeared.
DR MAYBLOOM: Roland, do you know how worried your teachers are? About you?
ROLAND: Only the Headmaster's upset. Mrs Walkham thought it was fantastic.
DR MAYBLOOM: And your parents. Very worried.
ROLAND: It's just the head—
DR MAYBLOOM: They're very, very concerned.
ROLAND: Are they?
DR MAYBLOOM: We need to be honest if we're going to make any progress. So I want you to think of me more like an old friend, not Dr Maybloom. Is that clear?
ROLAND: Progress?
DR MAYBLOOM: These imaginary people who are appearing.
ROLAND: They're not imaginary. They existed.
DR MAYBLOOM: And the first one was Alexander the Great.
ROLAND: Yes. He was real.
DR MAYBLOOM: Why Alexander? Do you have any idea?
ROLAND: I read a book about Alexander the Great that I got for my birthday, he did such great things, building an empire and he had this best friend called Hephaestion and they did everything together but his friend died and then Alexander died, he was still young, it was probably malaria which is a really stupid thing to die of when you've done so much, you get it from a mosquito bite and while I was thinking that, there he was.
DR MAYBLOOM: But you don't know how it happened?
ROLAND: No.
DR MAYBLOOM: You didn't make it happen?
ROLAND: No, he just turned up.
DR MAYBLOOM: I see. Tell me, what kind of books do you like reading?
ROLAND: Greek mythology. *The Iliad.*

DR MAYBLOOM: The what?

ROLAND: It's Homer. He was a Greek poet.

DR MAYBLOOM: I know who Homer was, but you read Greek literature?

ROLAND: They did a Classics Illustrated comic of *The Iliad*. *The Odyssey* too.

DR MAYBLOOM: And what do you like about Homer, Roland?

ROLAND: The battles. The heroes are really strong and fearless and they're nearly nude except for their armour which is blinding. They're packed in so tight together they can hardly fight. Their shields are jammed together and their swords are jammed together and then a spear will pierce a warrior's chest and his blood rushes out and he bites the dust. People say that about indians in westerns but that's where it comes from. Homer. 'He bit the dust and his shade fled.'

DR MAYBLOOM: How does that make you feel?

ROLAND: Sad.

DR MAYBLOOM: It makes you feel depressed?

ROLAND: No, sad.

DR MAYBLOOM: Why?

ROLAND: They're such great men but they still get speared and bite the dust. Men die on top of each other and that makes me feel...

DR MAYBLOOM: Yes? Tell me.

ROLAND: Sad.

DR MAYBLOOM: It makes you depressed. I see.

ROLAND: No, sad.

DR MAYBLOOM: Since then you've been able to make others appear?

ROLAND: Yes.

DR MAYBLOOM: How?

ROLAND: Thinking about them. They're people we read about in Social Studies and History.

DR MAYBLOOM: And do you feel the same about these others? Nurse Edith Cavell for instance, you feel sad about her?

ROLAND: 'Patriotism is not enough, I must have no hatred for anyone.' She was a very brave woman.

DR MAYBLOOM: She appeared in the classroom and then went outside and died in a hail of bullets. Your classmates were terrified.

ROLAND: They really liked it.

DR MAYBLOOM: Father Damien?

ROLAND: He gave his life to nursing people with leprosy.

DR MAYBLOOM: But was there any need to show your class the effects of the disease on Father Damien?

ROLAND: It's what happened to him.

DR MAYBLOOM: His nose fell off right in front of them.

ROLAND: They all clapped.

DR MAYBLOOM: Several mothers have complained their children are waking up in the night, screaming. Roland, we have to discover why this is happening. Now. These particular people. What do they have in common?

ROLAND: I don't really—

DR MAYBLOOM: They all died.

ROLAND: Yes.

DR MAYBLOOM: Yes. Violent or agonising deaths.

ROLAND: But they shouldn't have, they were good people, they did great things, they shouldn't have ended up like that, it seems… stupid.

DR MAYBLOOM: And that makes you feel?

ROLAND: Sad.

DR MAYBLOOM: You become depressed.

ROLAND: No, sad. Kind of sad. Good sad.

DR MAYBLOOM: Sadness is not a good thing to be feeling, Roland.

ROLAND: Isn't it?

DR MAYBLOOM: No it is not. [*Pause.*] Now, Roland, listen carefully. We have a word we use. The word is morbid. Sometimes young people have what are called morbid fantasies. And they can be very powerful, very exciting. But, we do have to grow out of them because if we don't, they can cause all sorts of problems when we grow up. Social problems, mental problems, what we call marital problems. So, from now on we'll be working very hard to prevent this alarming experience from ever happening again.

ROLAND: Do you mean it won't happen anymore?

DR MAYBLOOM: It will not, it will stop, as soon as we can make it stop.

ROLAND: But I don't want it to stop.

DR MAYBLOOM: It *is* a gift. Yes. But some gifts come from a very dark place and a gift like yours will have to be returned.

ROLAND: But it's great, everyone enjoys it when it happens and now everyone likes me and I've got lots of friends.

DR MAYBLOOM: This is Australia, 1966, Roland, not the Middle Ages. You'll have to work with me. We'll work together to find a cure!

ROLAND: I don't want a cure. I always want to be able to do it.

DR MAYBLOOM: You'll be free of this.

ROLAND: I don't want to be free of it.

DR MAYBLOOM: What's the matter, Roland? Why have you closed your eyes?

ROLAND: Thinking of someone. Joan of Arc. They burnt her at the stake. She heard voices that told her to save her people. She defeated the English. But they threw her in prison and tried her for being a witch.

An EXECUTIONER, *a hooded man with a flaming torch, approaches* DR MAYBLOOM.

And she was burnt at the stake.

DR MAYBLOOM *yells into his intercom.*

DR MAYBLOOM: Joyce, Joyce, get in here now! Roland make this stop!

ROLAND: No!

DR MAYBLOOM: Joyce call the fire brigade! And the police!

The HOODED MAN *vanishes.*

No, don't worry. No, I think we're all right. [*To* ROLAND] That's a terrible thing to do to someone. You could give a person a heart attack. What would your parents think if they knew what you'd done? Would they be proud that you'd nearly frightened someone half to death?

ROLAND: No.

DR MAYBLOOM: No, they would not. Sit down there. Now. We will force these horrid visions back down into the dark. For your sake, for your family's sake. First, your eyes must remain open, you must not let your mind wander where it will, in darkness. Next, if you feel these characters are about to appear, fix your gaze on something real and stare until you're thinking of nothing but the object in front of you and the feeling has passed. Try it now. Stare at this stapler. Stare. Harder. Tense, taut, like steel. Harder. Keep them away with all your might. Harder.

♦♦♦♦♦

MRS WALKHAM *finds* ROLAND *in a corner of the school playground.*

MRS WALKHAM: Roland, what's wrong? Why are staring at the ground like that, with your jaw clenched and your fists clenched?

ROLAND: The doctor said I mustn't let them come anymore. It's bad for me, it's bad for everyone, it's upsetting the other kids, even though they like what I do. I don't understand that. And my mother and father will worry and I don't want them to, they work hard so I'll be happy and normal. So I said yes I'd try to stop it happening. And now nobody likes me, no one talks to me. But sometimes I think I won't be able to stop it happening, no matter how hard I try.

MRS WALKHAM: Oh, Roland.

ROLAND: This morning when we were learning about Ludwig Leichhardt I kept thinking about him lost in the desert and he was almost here. I only just stopped him dying of thirst in front of everyone.

MRS WALKHAM: This is terrible.

ROLAND: I know.

MRS WALKHAM: What can I do to help?

ROLAND: I wish it would stop.

MRS WALKHAM: In my bag here I have a notebook and pencil. Perhaps, if you can whenever you feel they want to come, your special visitors, you could write it down. Here. Try to use the pencil and paper to empty your mind.

ROLAND: Yes.

MRS WALKHAM: Keep them with you all the time. Keep the pencil sharp. And whenever you feel one of them wants to appear, scribble it down.

ROLAND: Yes.

ROLAND *scribbles in the notebook.*

MRS WALKHAM: Yes, that's it, is that better?

ROLAND: I think so.

MRS WALKHAM: That's the boy.

She goes.

ROLAND: Thank you.

♦♦♦♦♦

ROLAND *is still scribbling, He's joined by* NICK EGLITIS.

NICK: What you writing?

ROLAND: Nothing.

NICK: I see you all the time, writing.

ROLAND: I have to. Keep writing.

NICK: Why?

ROLAND: Medical reasons.

NICK: You sick?

ROLAND: No.

NICK: You joking?

ROLAND: It's the truth. I can't really talk about it, why I have to write all the time.

NICK: Why you hiding down here?

ROLAND: Steve Gooding, he hits me. Whenever he sees me writing he hits me. So I come down here behind the woodwork block, so he won't see me.

NICK: Steve Gooding? Mr fucking Rugby Football? Good Aussie boy, can't write, can't read, can't think. Kicks fucking rugby ball. I stop him, he won't hurt you no more.

ROLAND: No, it's okay, I can hide down here.

NICK: No, he'll stop. I can't write much, not English. I would like to. At home we don't speak it. I would like to speak it good, read and write it. Like you. Hey, you know that English teacher, Miss Beverly, you know her?

ROLAND: Yeah. I'm in Miss Beverly's class, yes.

NICK: Yeah? Lucky man. Beautiful woman. I think of her at night, in bed, you know, Miss Beverly, Miss Beverly, Miss Beverly. Sorry, that was… sorry.

ROLAND: Her name's Joy.

NICK: Yeah. Joy, Joy, Joy, is better. I see her really clear, yeah, Joy, Joy, Joy. Thank you. My name is Nicolajs. Nick.

ROLAND: Roland. Roland.

NICK: Funny man. So, Roland the Writer, what's wrong with you?

ROLAND: You won't believe me.

NICK: Tell me.

ROLAND: This thing happens. For example. We'd been doing Antarctica in Geography and in the Maths class, I started thinking about Captain Scott, how he kept going to the South Pole and Titus Oates went out into the snow so he wouldn't be a burden and when I do that, what happens is—

TITUS OATES *staggers past.*

OATES: I'm just going outside. I may be some time.

ROLAND: There. See, it happened. I'm not supposed to let that happen. If I write it down, it keeps them away.

NICK: You made that happen? That guy?

ROLAND: Yes.

NICK: Fucking amazing.

NICK: Do it again.

ROLAND: It upsets people, gives them bad dreams.

NICK: Again.

ROLAND: The doctor said I mustn't.

NICK: Fuck the fucking doctor. It's fantastic, most fantastic thing I ever saw. Do it for me. I won't tell. A secret. For us.

♦♦♦♦♦

ROLAND*'s with* NINA *again.*

NINA: How was the week?

ROLAND: The week was very… interesting.

NINA: Unbelievable, yes. I nearly called you. I didn't of course, but… [*Pause.*] So. Do you want to talk about what happened?

ROLAND: Not especially.

Pause.

NINA: Okay. Good. So. Last time, we started talking about your friend. Nick.

ROLAND: Nicolajs Eglitis.

NINA: Yes. Do you want to talk more about him?

ROLAND: Sure.

Pause.

NINA: He was… Latvian?

ROLAND: That's correct.

Pause.

NINA: A new kid at school. He just turned up one day.

ROLAND: Yes.

NINA: And the only other person you shared your gift with.

ROLAND: Uh-huh.

NINA: Roland?

ROLAND: Yes.

NINA: You sure you don't want to talk about something else?

ROLAND: No. Not yet.

NINA: So… Nick.

ROLAND: Nick. He was older than me. He'd repeated a couple of years. His parents survived the war, they escaped the Russians. They lived in camps, they made it to Australia, lived in more camps and somehow they landed in Como and settled down to an ordinary suburban life.

♦♦♦♦♦

NICK *comes in, in hospital a gown, pushing a drip.*

NICK: This dream. Naked girls, me tied down, they come really close, nearly touching me, but I can't touch them, tied down. Wake up, wet, you know, everywhere. I get up, change the sheets, clean myself, back to bed and I'm still hard as rock. Wouldn't go down. I pull off, can't get anything out. Hours, hard and sore. Six o'clock, told my father. I couldn't stand up it hurt so much. He brought me straight here.

ROLAND: Is it better?

NICK: They gave me a needle, it went away. Now it obeys me. See. It's okay, you can look.

ROLAND: So when are you coming back to school?

NICK: When they know what it is.

ROLAND: When will that be?

NICK: When they get the results. Of the tests.

ROLAND: What tests?

NICK: They push a needle in your spine. It fucking hurts. And, Roland, look at my arms, they keep taking blood.

ROLAND: Bruises.

Pause.

NICK: So. What's happening at school?

ROLAND: Oh, you know.

NICK: Steve Gooding?

ROLAND: Yes.

NICK: He hit you?

ROLAND: Yes.

NICK: Bloody fucking bastard, I get out of here and I kill him. Fight back.

ROLAND: It's easier to get hit, less trouble. It's usually over pretty fast.

NICK: Bloody fucking rugby bastard. I should be there to stop him. I want to get out, I want to leave here.

He detaches the drip.

ROLAND: Nick! Don't!

STEVE: Why am I in this place? They don't know what's wrong with me. They don't know what to do with me. I want to get out of here. What if I never get out? I hate it here, I want to get out of here.

ROLAND: Nick, Nick, look.

MISS BEVERLY *comes in, wearing a very short mini skirt, reciting breathlessly.*

NICK: Ahhhh. Miss Beverly.

MISS BEVERLY: In delay there lies no plenty, then come kiss me, sweet and twenty, youth's a stuff will not endure, take me to you, imprison me, for I, except you enthral me, never shall be free, nor ever chaste, except you ravish me. Let us roll all our strength and all our sweetness up into one ball and tear our pleasures with rough strife, pillowed upon my fair love's ripening breast, to feel forever its soft fall and swell, awake forever in a sweet unrest, still, still to hear her tender-taken breath, and so live ever—or else swoon to death.

MISS BEVERLY *goes.*

NICK: Fucking amazing.

ROLAND: Yeah.

NICK: You can do real people now.

ROLAND: Yeah.

NICK: Living people.

ROLAND: Yeah.

Silence. A NURSE *comes in.*

NURSE: There you are, Nick. You should be back in bed. [*She sees the drip.*] Mislaid this, did you?

ROLAND: This is my friend Roland the Writer.

NURSE: Hello Roland the Writer.

ROLAND: Hullo.

NICK: This is Sister Shirley. Isn't she a beautiful woman?

ROLAND: Yes.

NURSE: Visiting hours are over.

ROLAND: Excuse me? Do you know when will Nick be going home?

NURSE: Yes I do. When he's better. And he won't get better if he's not allowed to rest. Two minutes.

The NURSE *goes.*

ROLAND: See. They don't know.
ROLAND: I'd better go. I'll see you later.
NICK: Promise me.
ROLAND: What?
NICK: Steve Gooding. Fight him. Do something to him. Promise.
ROLAND: I promise.

♦♦♦♦♦

A rugby football hits ROLAND *in the back. He turns to see who threw it.*

ROLAND: Steve Gooding, oh no.

He falls to the ground in a ball. STEVE GOODING *runs up, still in his sports gear.*

STEVE: Well, if it isn't the Como Homo. Get up. I can't hit you when you already on the ground.
ROLAND: I'm already late for Chemistry, can't you hit me in an hour?
STEVE: No, shut up.
ROLAND: You could just chuck my books on the bin, would that do?
STEVE: You can shove your fucking books up your fucken arse. Now, get up like I told you. Cat!

He hauls ROLAND *to his feet and drags him away from public view. They both see Roland's notebook has fallen from his pocket.*

STEVE *picks it up before* ROLAND *can get to it. He starts to leaf through it.* ROLAND *tries to get away but* STEVE *stops his exit.*

ROLAND *stands there helpless as* STEVE *reads.*

Oh ho ho. Here we go. 'Percy Bysshe Shelley has drowned and his body is being burned on the beach.' [*He tears the page out and throws it away.*] Oops. 'The Buddhist monk sits completely still while the flames turn his skin black.' [*He tears the page out and throws it away.*] Oops. 'Play practice. Miss Beverly knows everything about acting, she's brilliant.' [*Again the page torn out.*] Oops. 'The look on Steve Gooding's'… huh? [*He reads slower.*] 'The look on Steve Gooding's face when Lynette McKenzie's around. Total zombie. A line of drool drips from the corner of his mouth.'

ROLAND: I have to write down any stupid thing.

STEVE: 'Steve Gooding after the match. Taking his shirt off, his chest is wet with sweat and his legs are covered in mud and where his shorts…'

He reads to himself in silence for moment.

ROLAND: Whatever's in my head.

STEVE: I'm gunna kill you.

He grabs ROLAND.

ROLAND: It's for medical reasons, medical reasons!

STEVE: You'll never write another word.

ROLAND: Steve look, Lynette McKenzie.

LYNETTE *comes in.*

STEVE: Shut up. I'm gunna smash your head in.

ROLAND: It's Lynette!

STEVE: Holy shit! Lynette! Hang on. What's she doing here? Dressed like that?

ROLAND: She's ready for bed.

From left: Justine Clarke as Lynette, Richard Roxburgh as Roland and Russell Dykstra as Steve in the 2007 Company B production in Sydney. (Photo: Heidrun Löhr)

NICK: Huh? How come?
ROLAND: You like her Steve, don't you?
STEVE: Shut up. What's going on?
ROLAND: She's gorgeous.
STEVE: Yeah, she's gorgeous. But how come—?
ROLAND: Just relax and look at her.
STEVE: How is this happening?
ROLAND: Don't think about it, Steve.
STEVE: Lynette...
ROLAND: Tell me what you see.
STEVE: Her hair. Her mouth. Her...
ROLAND: Say it.
STEVE: Her tits.
ROLAND: She's sexy isn't she?
STEVE: She's fucken gorgeous.
ROLAND: You get a stiffy just looking at her?

He puts his hand on STEVE*'s cock.*

STEVE: What are you—?
ROLAND: Yeah, you like her don't you.

LYNETTE*'s gone.*

ROLAND: You can see her whenever you want.
STEVE: What do you mean?
ROLAND: Whenever you want. If you like.
STEVE: Lynette. Lynette.
ROLAND: Back of the woodwork block, half past three.
STEVE: Lynette...

STEVE *goes.*

♦♦♦♦♦

In the hospital. NICK *is frail.*

ROLAND: I met him there two times after school, but now he won't stop, every afternoon I'm at his place, in his bedroom.
NICK: You get him good.
ROLAND: 'Lynette, oooh Lynette.' It's like he's insane.
NICK: You made him crazy.
ROLAND: 'Oooh, Lynette.' He lets me do anything to him.

NICK: You, what, suck his dick?

ROLAND *nods.*

ROLAND: Anything. 'Oooh Lynette.'

NICK: You total pervert. Fantastic!

ROLAND: And. I've written a play. Miss Beverly wants to do something different for the end of term concert and she said I should write something. More than just scribbling. So I did. She's going to put it on. It's called *Toy Symphony*. It's a science fiction thriller. There's this flying English nanny who everyone thinks is really lovely but really, she's an alien, really cruel, evil. She lands in Como and starts giving all the kids lollies, but they're laced with a sleeping drug and she steals this kid and locks him in her spaceship. She's going to program his brain so he'll start killing everyone on her command. But this detective has been tracking her down, for other crimes in other places. He finds her spaceship and rescues the kid before she operates on him. He lets her go but he's planted a bomb on board and she takes off and as she's looking out the porthole and laughing at the world it explodes and she's annihilated. And as her body falls in pieces to the ground the school band's going to play Haydn's 'Toy Symphony'. The school band's going to play that at the end. And you have to be there. I'm writing it for you. You have to get better, so you can see it.

NICK: Bloody fucking genius.

ROLAND: You have to be there.

NICK: I will.

ROLAND: You will.

NICK: I'll be there.

♦♦♦♦♦

But the headmaster, MR DEVLIN, *has called* ROLAND *into his office.*

MR DEVLIN: Steve Gooding has been turning up late for training. His performance on the field has been lacklustre. He almost missed a vital game last week. Mr Fielding called him into his office after PE this morning and asked him what the matter was. Gooding broke down and confessed it all. Every sickening detail. The lad was sobbing. Steven Gooding is a school prefect, a popular student and a great footballer, the best this school has produced in all my time as Headmaster. Now, he's a wreck. And all because of you. What you have done is the most disgusting thing I've ever heard. Did you really think you could do this and not be found out? Did you really think a clean-living boy like Steve Gooding could keep a terrible secret shame like this to himself? And Gooding's father the leading businessman in the Shire. How am I expected to explain something like this happening in my school?

ROLAND: Sorry.

MR DEVLIN: Well, something has to give, you know that don't you? This play of yours that Miss Beverly's putting on. It's off for starters. Cancelled.

ROLAND: No, no, you can't, please.

MR DEVLIN: Just try and stop me. It sounds terrible anyway, this play, it's a send-up of *Mary Poppins*, which is a family picture everyone likes. But in your version she seems to be some sort of child molester.

ROLAND: It has to go on.

MR DEVLIN: The play is off. I confiscated all the copies from Miss Beverly this morning.

ROLAND: Please, Mr Devlin.

MR DEVLIN: I shoved them straight in the school incinerator. All of them. Burnt.

♦♦♦♦♦

NINA *has been listening to* ROLAND.

ROLAND: I didn't go to the hospital for two weeks, I didn't know how to tell Nick the play was cancelled. I rang his mother to see how he was. She put the phone down. I thought she was upset with me. His father came on and he was crying and he said, 'I'm sorry, Roland, but my son died last night', and he hung up.

Silence.

NINA: I'm sorry.

ROLAND *nods.*

Enormous impact on your life.

ROLAND *shrugs.*

You thought your play would help him get better?

ROLAND: I guess, in a way.

NINA: And because it was cancelled, you thought, was there a sense you'd…?

ROLAND: Failed him.

NINA: That's a tremendous burden. For someone so young. Did you write anything after that?

ROLAND: Nothing much, not until I was I don't know, late twenties.

NINA: And the… appearances? The gift?

ROLAND: Stopped. Gone.

Silence.

NINA: Roland?

ROLAND: Look.

Pause.

NINA: Tell me what's going through your mind. Right now.

ROLAND: You saw the news on the weekend?

NINA: Yes.

ROLAND: And?

NINA: Tell me, Roland.

ROLAND: *You* tell *me*.

NINA: Okay. The fires.

ROLAND: Bushfires.

NINA: Yes. Everywhere. Terrible weekend. The air filled with ash, burnt leaves.

ROLAND: The fires. Anywhere in particular?

NINA: Como.

ROLAND: And?

NINA: Burnt. Houses, churches. The school.

ROLAND: The school?

NINA: Your old school.

ROLAND: My old school.

NINA: Yes.

ROLAND: I spent my whole life explaining to people where I grew up and now they know it because it went up in smoke. Saturday, I turned on the television, there it was. Como. In flames. I rang my parents, they were already watching it. They don't live there anymore. But in a way they've never really left it. Our street, on fire. I went down to the beach, there was yes, ash falling out of the sky. Crowds of people watching this great column of smoke to the south. I stood there too, watching it, knowing what it was, the place, that place, a real place and a landscape in my mind, burning. And I felt nothing. That's when I thought, that's when I realised: time to let go. I'm not here to get it back, the writing, the whatever. I'm here to… closure, that's a word you like.

NINA: I hate that word.

ROLAND: Move on, let go—

NINA: I never use that language.

ROLAND: I have to stop wanting something back.

NINA: There's no reason that can't be part of the work we do, that option, the idea of… letting go, though I have to say I don't think that's where this is headed. But we can include it—

ROLAND: Nina, you've been… Coming here has been amazing. I kicked a nasty habit and for that alone—

NINA: Roland, we've been doing some great work and okay, it doesn't have an outcome yet, how could it? But there's so much more to explore, so much more of you to understand, to bring to the light.

ROLAND: Nina—

NINA: No, I don't want to throw it away now, on what, another hurdle? Which might lead somewhere important?

ROLAND: Just be patient?

NINA: Don't give in.

ROLAND: To the truth?

NINA: To despair.

ROLAND: Other writers have done it, accepted the loss. Wordsworth. Forster—

NINA: And O'Neill didn't and Fitzgerald didn't and Coleridge didn't.

ROLAND: I can live with it. Without it.

NINA: Really? Can you? Can you really?

ROLAND: And maybe I've just run out of things to write. There is that possibility.

NINA: Yes.

ROLAND: No one needs another writer flogging a dead horse and crying 'Poor me'. So I'm ready to let go.

NINA: Are you?

ROLAND: I… yeah.
NINA: You feel you've got to that, that's where you've—
ROLAND: Yes. Okay? I have to start to accept. So thank you.

Silence.

NINA: That's very…
ROLAND: Don't be upset.
NINA: Can't help it. Sorry.
ROLAND: And, thank you—
NINA: Sure.

ROLAND *stands to leave.*

And it's great you're that, completely certain.
ROLAND: It is.
NINA: That completely clear.
ROLAND: I will be.
NINA: I hope so. I really…

END OF ACT ONE

ACT TWO

A rehearsal room. ROLAND *comes in, sits, takes deep breaths, trying to calm himself.* DANIEL *comes in.*

DANIEL: Mr Henning? [*Pause.*] Mr Henning?

ROLAND: Yes?

DANIEL: Are you…?

ROLAND: I'm fine.

DANIEL: It's just that you left so fast, we were going to make a little speech, thanking you for coming to talk to us. [*Pause.*] Is anything, you look—

ROLAND: No. No. I just needed to…

DANIEL: So you're sure you're—

ROLAND: Yes.

DANIEL: I… Can I… I just wanted to say how much I enjoyed your talk. I really liked what you said. 'Film gives us substitute dreams, TV gives us substitute family, but theatre gives us genuine experience. The thing itself.' [*Pause.*] The thing. Itself.

ROLAND: Did I say that?

DANIEL: Yes. I really like that. That says it, that's what theatre does, yes. The thing itself. [*Pause.*] I admire you very much.

ROLAND: Uh-huh.

DANIEL: I just wanted to tell you that. I really like your work and I admire you. So…

Silence. DANIEL *goes to the door, almost leaves, but comes back.*

My name's Daniel.

ROLAND: Daniel.

DANIEL: Yes.

ROLAND: Great to meet you. Now…

DANIEL: You sure you don't need anything?

ROLAND: I'll be fine, left alone, thank you, and then I'll go to… somewhere I don't really want to go to but… I need… to go to.

DANIEL: I just don't want to leave you if—

ROLAND: You can.

DANIEL *stands there, waiting, watching.*

DANIEL: I'm in third year.

ROLAND: Uh-huh.

DANIEL: And then, well who knows?

ROLAND: You'll be an actor.

DANIEL: I think you need a job to call yourself that.

ROLAND: Well you just have to stay with it then, won't you? Persistence. You seem to have plenty of that.

DANIEL: You have to have a dream. Sounds cheesy but it's still true.

ROLAND: Well, you go on dreaming then, good luck.

ROLAND *goes on drawing deep breaths. He sees that* DANIEL *is still standing there.*

DANIEL: So… like I said I really—

ROLAND: You said it once, so there's no need to say it again, is there?

DANIEL: I just wanted you to know, I really admire—

ROLAND: Oh look—

DANIEL: —and respect, yes, I do.

ROLAND: Okay.

DANIEL: Yes. You have this, this gift.

ROLAND: Okay.

DANIEL: It's the truth, it is.

Silence. DANIEL *just keeps standing there. Finally…*

ROLAND: Okay, Daniel, so you're in third year.

DANIEL: Yes.

ROLAND: So what plays have you been in so far, while you've been learning to be an actor?

DANIEL: Well… I played the Poet in *Dreamplay* last year.

ROLAND: Strindberg?

DANIEL: It was a great experience.

ROLAND: Strindberg, Christ.

Pause.

DANIEL: We did scenes from *Faust*.

ROLAND: Now there's a boring play. Not even a play really.

DANIEL: *Peer Gynt*, we just did the last act.

ROLAND: Lucky for you.

DANIEL: And this year we're doing *Our Town*, I'm playing George Gibbs.

ROLAND: Awful play—

DANIEL: I'm looking forward to it—

ROLAND: Conservative, sentimental—

DANIEL: And I'm playing Ferdinand in *The Tempest* but you probably think that's a heap of shit as well.

DANIEL *laughs nervously, then stays standing there. Not leaving.*

ROLAND: You like doing plays?

DANIEL: I love it.

ROLAND: Do you?

DANIEL: Yes, God yes. The theatre.

ROLAND: What is it you like about *the* theatre?

DANIEL: Well… it's the most fantastic thing, it's like you said, the live thing, you're there in the room, with, it's sharing some experience, like people have done since whenever. The connection with the audience.

ROLAND: But. But. Don't you really want to be, really *really* want to be a movie star? Isn't that what you dream of?

DANIEL: I'd like to work in film.

ROLAND: But you just said you love *the* theatre. You can't do both.

DANIEL: Sure you can, you can do good work—

ROLAND: If you really love something you don't betray it. If you really loved *the* theatre you'd take a vow never, never to do anything but act on obscure stages hidden away from all publicity and work for a subsistence wage for the rest of your life with no hope of ever being in a smash hit, of being praised, of even being noticed and you would keep that vow with the fervour of a saint.

DANIEL: That would be, that's a pretty intense—

ROLAND: Too demanding?

DANIEL: It'd be nice to have a reasonably, you know, a bit of comfort wouldn't be—

ROLAND: So you don't want art, you want lifestyle, you want to be on the cover of *Who Weekly* and go to film festivals for free and get into nightclubs without queuing and have Annie Liebowitz take your photo for *Vanity Fair* and make documentaries about shooting your new film where you talk earnestly about how a bunch of pricks you despised totally were great to work with and how generous they were and how privileged you were—

DANIEL: Okay, look—

ROLAND: Not true?

Pause.

DANIEL: Okay, yes, I suppose, there's a part of me, a part of anyone, recognition, free of worrying about money. We all want that I reckon. I'm sorry if that's bad, it's selling out or something. Maybe I've read too many *Vanity Fairs*.

He laughs again.

ROLAND: Why did you follow me in here?

DANIEL: I didn't, I didn't follow you.

ROLAND: Yeah you did.

DANIEL: You left fast, walked out, I wanted to thank you.

ROLAND: That's all?

DANIEL: Um. Yes. Yes, that's all.

ROLAND: But you don't want anything else?

DANIEL: Um. No.

ROLAND: Something else, something extra?

DANIEL *thinks.*

DANIEL: If I was honest, I suppose… now I'm here… advice? No. Insight. Maybe I'd like some insight, into it all, theatre, acting? Something for someone like me to hang on to. In this, in it all. Some… clue?

ROLAND: Clue.

DANIEL: Some… yes. Clue. Hint?

ROLAND: And you think I'd have that?

DANIEL: Yes. You would. Definitely.

Pause.

ROLAND: Let's get out of here.

DANIEL: Now?

ROLAND: I'm really hungry, listening to you has made me hungry. Let's get out of here. Let's eat, a drink.

DANIEL: I can't.

ROLAND: You want a clue, a hint.

DANIEL: But. Now?

ROLAND: Let's get a cab and go somewhere?

DANIEL: Mr Henning, it's really terrific—

ROLAND: What if I'm about to give you the clue? Right now. You going to throw it away because why, you've got to go to class and pretend to be a tree?

DANIEL: I can't just—

ROLAND: Take a leap. Now, right now, just let's get out of here.

DANIEL: Man. I…

ROLAND: Jump. Let's go. All the clues you want. I'm better than any class you'll get here.

DANIEL: And… well… what do you get?

ROLAND: Me?

DANIEL: What do you get out of this?

ROLAND: As much as I can.

DANIEL: Okay, see, I'm not really—

ROLAND: How do you know, Daniel? How can you know at your age, what, twenty-three?

DANIEL: Four, twenty-four—

ROLAND: You want to be an actor and you can't take one single, simple leap into the unknown for an afternoon?

DANIEL: See I just don't feel comfortable—

ROLAND: But that's why you're here. That's why you followed me.

DANIEL: No. I came in here to thank you for your talk.

ROLAND: No. You followed me in here to make a big impression.

DANIEL: No, I swear, that's not—

ROLAND: Roland Henning likes young men, it's well known, no secret, they've probably got some database here with the names of everyone who might be of use. Then you made a plan: push yourself into his consciousness and if he ever writes a part you might be right for he'll think of you. I did see you up the back, by the way, with your legs spread just far enough to give me a view up those baggy shorts. Thank me? This is a career move. I bet they teach you that as well, in between the mime classes and fencing lessons and The World's Most Boring Plays and how to cry on cue? Well this is your day, you're in luck, Daniel, I'm here to be impressed.

DANIEL: No, no, no—

ROLAND: I'm here to make your day. I'll just get my dick out and you can suck me off right here in this classroom.

DANIEL: I wouldn't, I would never—

ROLAND: Come on, I'm ready, let's get to it. Or you want *me* to kneel down for *you*, that the deal? Don't worry, Daniel, it's an old story, time honoured, been around since Aeschylus was a boy.

DANIEL: You're so wrong.

ROLAND: Can you honestly say that? I'm wrong? Do you know so little about yourself? Why you do what you do? What kind of an actor are you going to make if you can't even figure out why you came in here?

DANIEL: This is too… I never—

ROLAND: I'm going to count to three, Daniel. You can choose. Come with me now, see where it goes, what you can do, what experience you can find. And you'll get the full download, from the horse's mouth, the inside tip, the backstage pass to a playwright's innermost workings. Or. Stay here and become a soapie star. Not so bad. There's money, a bit of glamour. At least some decent coke. Your choice, Dan. One. Think about what you'll miss out on. Or what you might get.

DANIEL: Yeah and you get—

ROLAND: I get something unexpected, unforeseen, something crazy. Something to write about. Something. To write about. Yeah, I'll write something, with a part for you. What an offer. A part written for you with all the insight you want. Imagine that. Two.

DANIEL: I…

ROLAND: When you came in here I was getting ready to go the hospital. To see my father. He's been sick you see, for years, but now he's in the final stretch. I've slowly been losing everything I write, I wrote about, what drove me to write, the whole well is being filled in. That's why I left the room in a hurry. I heard myself saying all that stuff about writing to you all, sitting there, some of you were even taking notes and I thought 'You fake, you're a fake, you might never write again. There'll be nothing left.' So I had to get out. But here you are, wanting a clue and I'm happy to grab anything that might spur me on. Let's help each other out. How you doing, Daniel, made up your mind?

Silence.

Three. That's it. Time to go. But I will leave you with something. Here's an insight. A clue. Your career as an actor? Learn to make a decent coffee.

♦♦♦♦♦

ROLAND*'s at home, on the phone to his friend Jake.*

ROLAND: No Jake, I didn't go on at them, wasn't ranting at them, that's not the point.

I was trying to tell you what happened today, at the funeral. Look. Look, Jake, you want me to tell you? Okay.

This is what happened. I was standing at the lectern, reading what I'd written about my mother. The funeral was in the church they were married in, right? I looked down the aisle and while I was speaking I thought I could see my mother and father, walking up the aisle on their wedding day, walking towards me. And then and *then* I was seeing me leading my mother down that same aisle, following my father's coffin and how that day I'd been thinking 'I'm walking my mother down the aisle like my father led her down the aisle sixty years ago, almost exactly sixty years ago, it was summer, it was really hot.' And here we were only six weeks after *that* and I'm standing in the same church, the same people are sitting looking at me, listening, and here's my *mother* lying in *her* coffin just behind me. And I, I just started thinking, while I was reading what I'd written about her, I was thinking about everything people had been saying to me, their friends, the minister—everything I'd heard for the whole week. I started to—I was denying it, in my head, thinking 'I'm sorry I *don't* think they're happy at last, I *don't* think they're together again, forever, I don't *buy* that. First, what does that say about the life we have? That it's just the prelude to the real thing, which will be just the good bits of this life going on forever? Is that all this is, a warm-up, a test run, an entrée platter of tastes of things to come? That's pretty, that's pretty trivial, how inane is that?' I was talking on, reading the eulogy, but in my mind I was asking 'Isn't it presumptuous? How do we *know* that's all there is, this life here, the life we know and then another one on the other side of death? There might be more, so much more, somewhere else, other lives, many, many other lives. If we're going to talk about there *being* somewhere else, if we're going to go that far, why should there be, how do we know there's only two, here and hereafter, why not here and there and there and everywhere? Lots of places where it's just as hard in other ways. There's hardships other parts of us have to endure. Isn't that what we should be talking about? My parents dream, right, was a suburban paradise where life was just supposed to get better and better without end but it ended in hospitals and pain and despair and panic and fear. That dream was squeezed out of them until they saw that life was merciless. And it is, clearly. He spent a decade in hell with the strokes and he couldn't talk and then two years to die with the cancer. She nursed him for ten years, her life shrinking down to his bedside then she just crashed and burnt with *her* cancer. They learnt there's a tar pit and in the end we all blunder into it. And in they went, but even as they sank they never gave up, never stopped struggling against pain and fear and humiliation and doctors. They were so good at it, fighting even as they sank. So why should we want them to give up now, where there's so much more to fight in these other worlds, if that's what we want to believe. Don't trivialise them, let's not think of them sitting around drinking tea or gardening in the blessed fields forever, not yet, no. Let's wish them all the luck they can find for the next horror stretch, let's hope they get to burn off more, to dig deeper, to wrestle even crueller angels because we know they were good wrestlers and that they might find meaning not in God's eternal undercover shopping mall but in making the way easier for us, slaying a few demons before we get there.'

And the minister, he must have shifted in his pew, or coughed or something. I looked at him, he was staring at me really hard, I looked at everyone else, they were all staring and… Well, I wasn't thinking any of that. I'd been saying it. It had come out. Of my mouth. Out loud.

So then I stopped, I was suddenly dizzy. The minister, poor guy, he stood up and took my arm and led me back to the pew and they were all thinking 'the strain, the grief, poor Roland'. We went back to the script, bit of music, a prayer, and yes, grief, yes, and all I could hear was the traffic in the street outside and thinking about them getting into that big black car sixty years ago and driving off to live their dream together in Como and now there's another big black car waiting to take her body to be burned like a big black car took *his* body to be burned six weeks ago.

The point? Of what I said? I don't know, but what I said was at least interesting, but the point?

Writing? No. Because… Well, you know what? You'd think a writer could make something out of this.

But I can't be bothered. I have this really strong feeling, you see, that I'm meant to follow them. That they're waiting for me and that I'm meant to join them and everything else is a waste of time, stopping me from going after them.

No don't come home. I'm really—

No there's no need for you to come home. No. Absolutely.

I won't do anything like that, I won't. No. Promise.

I can hear a siren.

A New York siren.

It's great that you worry. Yes. You're the best, you are. My best…

I will. Love to Alison. I will.

Goodnight.

Goodnight Jake. Yes.

Me too.

Goodnight.

♦♦♦♦♦

ROLAND*'s with his former dealer,* TOM.

TOM: So no one saw you downstairs?

ROLAND: No one.

TOM: No one saw you at the intercom?

ROLAND: No.

TOM: Good, that's good.

ROLAND: Tom, I'm sorry if I've come at a bad time but I won't stay long.

TOM: Bad time? After how long?

ROLAND: It has been a while, I know.

TOM: A while?

ROLAND: But you're still here, same address, fantastic. Things have been a little, I just wanted to see you.

TOM: *Needed* to see me.

ROLAND: Well I just, I just walked over, buzzed your number and you're still here.

TOM: *Needed* to see me.

ROLAND: I suppose.

TOM: To score.

ROLAND: Well, if you're going to call a spade a... yeah, okay. I really, look, Tom, I'm really, I don't need much, just something to calm me down, slow me down, just a bit, that's all.

TOM: But you see I don't think that will be possible. Since, for some reason, you no longer required my services and you just vanished.

ROLAND: Yes. Things changed. I stopped using.

TOM: Right, so you stopped?

ROLAND: I did. Eventually.

TOM: Just cold turkey stopped?

ROLAND: I had help but yes, cold turkey. Look, Tom, I stopped. I thought if I cleaned myself up things would start working for me again.

TOM: And they did.

ROLAND: And they did, yes, but now, well...

TOM: So now you want to feel good again and thought you'd come and see your old mate Tom.

ROLAND: Yes.

TOM: There was never anything wrong with what you were getting here, was there?

ROLAND: No, there was never a problem with what you were giving me, none. Did I ever give you that—?

TOM: It wasn't rubbish I was you giving you, was it, not baby powder or rat poison? It was cut straight off the rock—

ROLAND: It was great.

TOM: I always threw in something extra. Something to smoke, something to keep you going, or bring you back down.

ROLAND: It wasn't anything... There was nothing wrong... You did.

TOM: And I'm not some scabby junkie in a lane, am I?

ROLAND: No, no you're not, of course not.

TOM: It was always safe here, discrete, friendly. I provided an excellent service, I'd say. I even home delivered upon request.

ROLAND: You did yes. You were, I couldn't fault what you were doing for me and you helped me. I stopped feeling sad and hopeless and alone and empty and you did that for me.

TOM: Yeah, thanks, great, but like you said. Things change. For instance, you want to feel better again and I'm supposed to provide the same service I gave you before. But I so don't care because I, well I don't have to put up with it, I won't be, you won't treat me like that. And now I don't want to do business. At your convenience. So you should just go.

ROLAND: Oh Tom, no, come on, look I apologised.

TOM: You should just go.

Pause.

ROLAND: It hasn't been so good lately.

TOM: I really don't—

ROLAND: It's not just—

TOM: I so don't care.

ROLAND: My family, well, actually I don't have a family anymore. Since my mother died I've tried to keep going, but I'm not doing well. At all.

TOM: Nothing to do with me, never was, really, but now, don't care. You should just—

A phone rings. TOM*'s a bit thrown but covers.*

Excuse me.

He finally picks up.

Hi matey. Yeah. Sure. See you soon.

He ends the call.

ROLAND: Is someone coming?

TOM: Yeah.

ROLAND: I can be gone really fast, just let's—

TOM: No.

ROLAND: Tom.

TOM: No.

ROLAND: I… please…

Pause.

TOM: Look, it's Josh. Okay? So, piss off.

ROLAND: Josh?

TOM: Yeah. I've got him for a week. It's a kind of trial thing. His mother is going to leave him with me. She's on her way over with him. Okay? Now you know. So—

ROLAND: Josh? With you? Tom, that's great. It'll be great for both of you. He must be…?

TOM: Seven last month.

ROLAND: Fantastic. He's a great kid.

TOM: He is.

ROLAND: Oh, that's why you were worried about me turning up, her seeing me buzzing you downstairs.

TOM: Basically.

ROLAND: Because if there's anything going on here when she brings him up, he won't be here five minutes, she'll be out the door with him if she thinks there's anything going down. Right. So. Easy. I'll get what I came for and I'll be gone.

TOM: Look, look, really, I don't have anything, I got rid of it, out of my life, I stopped, because of Josh.

ROLAND: Nothing?

TOM: Good. I'm glad you understand.

ROLAND: I do. I do. It's great about Josh.

TOM: Yeah. So, if you don't mind?

ROLAND: It's a big day for you.

TOM: Yes it is, big day. So… [*Pause.*] There's nothing here. God's truth.

ROLAND *sits.*

Oh, come on man…

ROLAND: You know, all that time ago, before I, like you said, vanished, you helped me, you did, you did help me feel better, you did. There were some great nights, down on the beach or up on McKenzie's Point, just skimming out there to the horizon. I stopped feeling worthless, useless, I felt capable, brave, full of ideas. Yes, I felt good. But it was all. Crap. When you're feeling great, it's not you feeling great, it's those damn drugs feeling great, every thought, every idea, every insight, isn't worth the synapse it's written on. So yeah you helped me feel great but it was a big lie. So 'I'm really sorry I dropped out of your life, I'm sorry I turned my back on your top notch service with its customer-focused vision, I'm sorry I tried to get my mind back by foregoing the high quality product you were moving', isn't really the point here. I've had it. Pussy's bow, darling. So on one hand there's me, ready and willing to start my own slide down into the tar pit, using your superior brand product. And then, on the other hand, there's you. You've got your little boy on his way over with his mother who mustn't know I'm here. Or why I'm here.

TOM: Fuck man, this is great, fucking great.

ROLAND: So thanks for getting me to grovel, it was an interesting experience, begging forgiveness from my *dealer*. And giving me all your outrage because I disappeared from your life which was all just to get me out of here so your little boy'll never know his dad's a *dealer*. But Tom. I'm not budging. You must have something here. Look at you, shaking like a lamb at the altar, you can't tell me you haven't got something here somewhere, to get you through this, keep you together through this highly stressful time. So. Tom, I'll go. If you want me to, if you don't want her to know I'm here. But not with empty hands am I going.

Pause. The intercom buzzes. TOM *jumps.*

TOM: Jesus man.

ROLAND: 'Jesus man.' And I don't just want something to calm me down. I want the lot. Tom, I'm here to help, I'll take it all off your hands. I'm looking to buy up like Christmas.

ROLAND *shows* TOM *his wallet. Pause.*

Kids are expensive these days, the things they need.

The buzzer goes for several seconds.

TOM: You're a fucking arsehole.

ROLAND: What are you going to do? Throw me out? Kill me? Call the fuzz—?

TOM: I'll give you what I've got.

ROLAND: There you go.

TOM *goes.* ROLAND *calls after him.*

Look. Keep a bit back, you don't want to lose it in the middle of this big week. And nothing will happen, I'll go, she won't know, I'll duck down one floor, wait until she's up here.

TOM *comes back in and hands* ROLAND *a small backpack.*

Tell her you were in the shower, she'll—

TOM *picks up the handset.*

TOM: Yeah, sorry, how are you, in the shower. Come on up.

ROLAND: You're going to have a great time with him. [*He gets up to leave.*] And wet your hair so she believes you.

♦♦♦♦♦

Roland's place. He's just got home.

He takes a plastic bag full of white powder out of the backpack. He opens it, tastes its bitterness. MRS WALKHAM *comes back.*

MRS WALKHAM: Now. Interesting fact. Our little suburb was known to some great writers. At the end of his life, Henry Lawson was living in a hut in the bend of the Woronora River call The Bonnet. Dame Mary Gilmore herself, a great Australian poet, visited Lawson here. He was ill, drinking, destroying his health, his talent. Such a sad end.

And in February 1922, D. H. Lawrence and his wife Frieda sailed from Europe on their way, eventually, to America. Lawrence was sick of Europe, sick of the waste of the First World War, sick of the problems caused by his books, *The Rainbow* was actually withdrawn from publication and destroyed. And he'd made enemies because he'd put people he knew in his books, he'd lost friends. The Lawrences went first to Ceylon, to visit friends there. But he hated the heat and couldn't write, so he and Frieda came to Australia.

ROLAND *has put some powder on the side of his hand. He snorts it, then packs a cone with a lot of coke sprinkled on it.*

Sydney was too expensive for them to live, so they found a little cottage in Thirroul, on the coast south of Sydney. And here Lawrence actually began to write again. And of course, to get to Thirroul, they would have taken the train, which would have crossed the Georges River at Como.

The coke kicks in.

And we know they passed through Como, because when Lawrence turned his time in this country into a book, called *Kangaroo*, he wrote, at the beginning of Chapter Five, I've marked the passage, here it is: 'Como said the station sign. And they ran on bridges over two arms of water from the sea, and they saw what looked like a long lake with wooded shores and bungalows: a bit like Lake Como, but oh, so unlike. That curious sombreness of Australia, the sense of oldness, with the forms all worn down low and blunt, squat. The squat seeming earth.' So there it is, our little suburb, in a famous English writer's work.

ROLAND: This stuff is intense.

MRS WALKHAM: You shouldn't do this.

ROLAND: Don't give me a pep talk.

MRS WALKHAM: You really shouldn't.

ROLAND: I saw this shrink once. She said, this woman I was seeing, she said she wanted me to find clarity. But what I need is lack of clarity. I need, darkness. Obscurity. I want the light turned off, not up.

MRS WALKHAM: Isn't there something you were going to do tonight?

ROLAND: No, go away.

MRS WALKHAM: Why is that school case sitting there?

ROLAND: That?

MRS WALKHAM: It's yours. It's got your name written on the inside of the lid, doesn't it?

ROLAND: Probably.

MRS WALKHAM: It does, I remember.

ROLAND: Yes.

MRS WALKHAM: What's in it?

ROLAND: Paper.

MRS WALKHAM: What paper?

ROLAND: My mother kept papers in it.

MRS WALKHAM: What kind of papers?

ROLAND: Life papers. Insurance, passports, pension books—Why am I talking to you? Go back to whatever vault… down there with Jacob Marley and Hamlet's father, go on.

MRS WALKHAM: Aren't you going to look?

ROLAND: Not right now.

MRS WALKHAM: Why not?

ROLAND: I'll go through it when I'm ready.

MRS WALKHAM: You're ready now.

ROLAND: Will you lay off?

MRS WALKHAM: Are you afraid of what's in it?

ROLAND: No, it's just a relic. I'm a bit tired of relics, just now, tired of the past, had enough.

MRS WALKHAM: You're an orphan, yes, it's hard. Facing the past, the loss. There were always the three of you and now there's just you.

ROLAND: Shut up, okay, here. Look… I'm opening it. There's an envelope with birth certificates. There's the house insurance. Passports. Deeds to the house. You see, not so tough. Old bank books. Cheque book stubs, years of them. School photos.

MRS WALKHAM: There's me. With 5A. There you are.
ROLAND: So it is. Every class. High school.
MRS WALKHAM: There's your friend Nick.
ROLAND: So it is.
MRS WALKHAM: And what's in that envelope?
ROLAND: This?
MRS WALKHAM: Open it up.
ROLAND: Why?
MRS WALKHAM: Go on. Open it.

ROLAND *takes out an envelope, opens it, and takes out a handwritten script.*

You recognise it? It's your writing.
ROLAND: It is.
MRS WALKHAM: You remember what it is?
ROLAND: Yes. How did it get here?
MRS WALKHAM: Long time ago.
ROLAND: But I thought they were all destroyed. Burnt.
MRS WALKHAM: Not all of them.
ROLAND: Someone must have sent it to Mum. She never told me.
MRS WALKHAM: She just kept it.

Silence. He looks at the script.

ROLAND: Did she ever read it?
MRS WALKHAM: Goodness knows. But she kept it. It was precious, she knew that.
ROLAND: This old play.

♦♦♦♦♦

MRS WALKHAM *brings an assortment of instruments onstage and accompanies the play with her own version of Haydn's 'Toy Symphony', supported by whatever kind of recorded or live sound is appropriate.* ROLAND *watches the performance.*

A rocket lands and an English NANNY, *floats down from it with her umbrella unfurled. Two young* BOYS *run to greet her. She gives them sweets. One of the boys, slower to unwrap his, watches in horror as the other boy convulses and foams as soon as he has swallowed his lolly. The surviving boy runs off in terror.*

The NANNY *works on the other boy, now stupefied. He twitches and spasms as she uses her umbrella to rewire his brain.*

A DETECTIVE *comes in. He sees the* NANNY *at work and rushes to stop her. She fights him off, they struggle, he overpowers her and she falls in a heap in a corner.*

The DETECTIVE *uses this opportunity to hide a bomb on the Nanny's rocket.*

Recovered, the NANNY *repulses the* DETECTIVE *and the rocket takes off. As it leaves the earth, the* DETECTIVE *presses the button in his remote device and the rocket explodes. The* NANNY *is annihilated in a burst of light.*

♦♦♦♦♦

A bar. DANIEL*'s there with* ROLAND. *They both have drinks.*

ROLAND: First. Thank you for coming, thank you for agreeing to see me.
DANIEL: Can I—?

From left: Guy Edmonds as a Boy, Justine Clarke as the Nanny and Russell Dykstra as a Boy in the 2007 Company B production in Sydney. (Photo: Heidrun Löhr)

ROLAND: No, wait, it was good of you.
DANIEL: Sorry, but can I—?
ROLAND: Do you mind, I just want to say this—
DANIEL: But you see, really I don't—
ROLAND: I was relieved—
DANIEL: Can I speak?
ROLAND: No, Daniel, please—
DANIEL: No? No? I can't talk? After what's happened with us so far I reckon the best thing you can do is shut up, just shut up okay, and listen.
ROLAND: Yes.
DANIEL: You said, what you said that day, the things you said, after you left, you know, I was reeling. You made me doubt everything, everything I was doing. I got so, I could hardly get out of bed. But I had to get through it, I was, in the end, determined to get through it. So I thought really, really hard 'Well, is what he said true?' Otherwise… And this is where I got to. Yes, I need to get braver, I need to take a leap. I said that day 'I'm not comfortable'. Well, who wants to see a play or, yes, a *movie* about people being comfortable? And yes. I'm not, I need to understand what drives me, what my motivation is. And be honest about that, even if it's not what someone wants to hear. Like, I heard about your parents and was going to send you a card. But then I thought 'Why am I doing this? Really. Is there something I'm not admitting, is it some *plan*?' But no, why was I going to send a card? Because I was sorry. That was the truth. Then all these months later you ask me to come here and see you and I think 'Okay I'll go', but then I nearly don't because I'm thinking 'Why are you going? *Really*.' Answer, I want to see you to get this off my chest, to tell you what I've been through.
ROLAND: Daniel—
DANIEL: If I can't be honest, how can I play a human being who wants, at this moment wants, whatever? If I don't know exactly what that's like, I'm, like you said, I'm a fake. I should give up right now. So you were in a really bad place that day, but I needed to hear it, I needed to hear what you had to say. I wanted some, some insight, some clue. And in spite of everything I got what I wanted. So, thank you. That's the truth. Thank. You. I mean it's tragic really, acting student. All the hard work and like you said, 'What if you spend your life doing

soaps? After all you've been through will you ever play Hamlet or do Chekhov? Or maybe land a dog food commercial? If you're lucky.' All you look for is some bit of inspiration, some little thing that'll help you keep going, keep turning up and… So. Thank you.

Pause.

ROLAND: That's…

DANIEL: Clumsy and stupid and remedial.

ROLAND: No. No. Okay. Daniel. I didn't want to just say sorry, not just *say* it. It's like, for us, between us, I've ruined words. So I want to *do* something, that would be better than words. I want to give you something. I found this, in an old case, full of my parents' stuff. I didn't know it was there, no idea. It's this play I wrote when I was a kid. It never went on, it got cancelled, banned I guess, as a punishment. The school Headmaster had all the copies burnt. But one minute I was looking through deeds and insurance policies and the next. Here it was. This thing I wrote. So here.

DANIEL: No, I can't.

ROLAND: My English teacher, Miss Beverly, must have sent it to my mother. She must have had no idea what it was, what it was about, what it meant, but because a teacher said keep it, she did. I want you to have it.

DANIEL: No way.

ROLAND: No. It's nothing, it's just a skit a twelve-year-old wrote, but somehow, you having it would, it would make me feel better. So.

DANIEL: This is… this is awesome.

ROLAND: You'll take it?

DANIEL: But it, this is worth money.

ROLAND: Maybe, not much. So you'll take it?

DANIEL: Really?

ROLAND: Yes.

DANIEL: Awesome.

ROLAND: Not particularly.

DANIEL: No, no. I'll look after it like it was… like it was in the British Museum or somewhere, with the glass cases where you see all the… the…

ROLAND: Well.

DANIEL: Yes. In a special place, I don't know, a special… container. Or something.

ROLAND: Good.
DANIEL: And I swear, I will never, this will never be on eBay.
ROLAND: If you need to, Daniel, one day, starving actor you might need to.
DANIEL: Never.

Silence.

This is a great view. Great place to just sit. No one on the beach. Water looks cold.

ANTON CHEKHOV *appears.*

CHEKHOV: [*in Russian*] *Dobre utro. Proshu velikodushno prostit menya. Za to chto perebivaju vashu besedu. Prosto ja hotel bi skazatvam. Molodoy chelovek. O svojey zadumke napisat chayku. Gde bi vi sigrali rol.* [Good morning. Please forgive my interrupting you, but I wanted to tell you, young man, that I feel that I could have written *Seagull* with you in mind.]
DANIEL: I'm sorry I don't speak— [*To* ROLAND] Is this Russian—?
ROLAND: Yes.
CHEKHOV: [*in Russian*] *Munnyeah car sjetssa. Boota rol Konstatina Treplerva, ya nappysal. Tlya vas Orchen preyatno sevo ha ro sha va.* [It's as if I wrote the role of Konstantin Treplev for you. It is an honour to meet you. Good day to you both.]

CHEKHOV *goes again. Silence.*

DANIEL: Did you know him?
ROLAND: Well…
DANIEL: You know who he looked like?
ROLAND: Yes.
DANIEL: Chekhov, right? Looked like him I mean, right?
ROLAND: He did, yes.
DANIEL: What was he saying?
ROLAND: I'm not…
DANIEL: Did he say Konstantin?
ROLAND: Konstantin Treplev, I think so, yes.
DANIEL: The guy in *The Seagull*, the playwright, the young guy.
ROLAND: Uh-huh.
DANIEL: So who *was* that?
ROLAND: Well…

DANIEL: Maybe he was saying something about me playing that role.
ROLAND: Maybe.
DANIEL: Weird, and I was just talking about Chekhov.
ROLAND: And I was just thinking about him.
DANIEL: Really?
ROLAND: Just then.
DANIEL: Weird. [*Pause.*] Huh. We should get another drink. To toast this. Sitting in a bar with a writer and Chekhov just turns up. We should raise a glass. You want another…?
ROLAND: Yes, thank you.
DANIEL: Same?
ROLAND: Yes.
DANIEL: Sure. Chekhov? Huh. Awesome.

THE END

Also by Michael Gow and available from Currency Press

All Stops Out
978 0 86819 310 6

Away
978 0 86819 211 6

Europe / On Top of the World
978 0 86819 158 4

The Fortunes of Richard Mahony (from the novel by Henry Handel Richardson)
978 0 86819 678 7

Furious
978 0 86819 362 5

The Kid
978 0 86819 833 0

Sweet Phoebe
978 0 86819 430 1